KU-739-225

EASY DESIGN
ON YOUR COMPUTER

using *only* Microsoft® Word 2000 or
Microsoft® Office 2000

Anna Claybourne

Designed by Isaac Quaye
Cover design by Russell Punter

Edited by Jane Chisholm and Philippa Wingate
Design manager: Russell Punter
Illustrated by Isaac Quaye
Photographs by Howard Allman

Technical consultant: Janette Bailey
Design consultant: Biggles

This is a product of Usborne Publishing Ltd., and is not sponsored by
or produced in association with Microsoft Corporation.

TED SMART

What does easy design mean?

Contents

This book is all about how you can design and produce your own publications ~ from cards and books to T-shirts, stickers and stationery ~ using only a computer and Microsoft® Word 2000.

It's easy because you don't need to be a design genius or brilliant at art to put words and pictures together to make effective, eyecatching designs.

Why design?

Design influences everything. Whether you're trying to create a birthday card, poster, magazine, newsletter or school project, the way it looks can make all the difference. The design you choose decides whether something comes across as funny, exciting, serious or sophisticated. If a design doesn't work, it can end up looking dull, old-fashioned ~ or just silly.

This book is about graphic design ~ the kind of design that deals with words and pictures. Today, most graphic designers work on computers. Doing graphic design on a computer is sometimes called desktop design or desktop publishing (DTP for short).

Computers make designing easier, because you can rearrange things as much as you like on the screen. Then, when you've finished, you can print out as many copies as you want.

Make your own unique greetings cards and invitations.

Happy Birthday

Design software

Most professional graphic designers use special DTP software. However, this is usually very expensive, and as a beginner you probably won't need it. This book shows you how to get great results using a less expensive word-processing program, Microsoft® Word 2000.

You can publish books and newsletters for friends and family.

Grandpa George turns 100!

After a century of studying sea creatures, fighting in World Wars and drinking a lot of tea, Grandpa George will celebrate his 100th birthday on Thursday 5 April.

Don't miss the party!

A birthday garden party will be held at George's house in Birmingham on Saturday 7 April. All Edwards family members are invited.

The party is being organized by Millie Edwards, George's great niece. E-mail Millie at MillieE@usborne.co.uk, or phone her on 098 765 4321, for all the details.

Bob and Becky's big b bonanza

On February 12, Bob Edwa his wife Becky were blesse not one, not two, but thre little girls! Everything went the triplets were born just midnight. The bouncing b been named Bridget, Britn Blodwen.

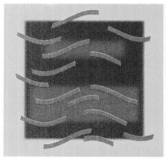

MY BOOK OF POEMS

Find out how to create interesting lettering styles.

You could put your designs onto clothes, wrapping paper, stickers and badges.

How this book works

This book has been divided into three sections to make it easy to use.

• The **Getting Started** section deals with all the equipment and software you need to get going, and explains the basics of good design.

• The main section, **Working with Word**, shows you all the different ways you can use Word 2000 as a design tool. Each double page introduces a new skill, such as adding pictures, choosing lettering styles or arranging text and pictures on the page. With each new skill, there's a new project to try. This will help you build up your design skills step-by-step. But you don't need to work through every project, especially if you've used Word before.

• The **Going Further** section, at the end of the book, is about DTP software. It gives you a brief introduction to the way professional designers work and the programs they use.

Design tips

Look out for "design tips" boxes like this throughout the book. They'll give you extra ideas and suggestions to help with particular projects.

You can print out personalized stationery featuring your own logo.

The Cherry Tree Café
10 Cherry Tree Way, Jedley

Marina Fish • 14 Seaview S
marina@webnet.com

Dawn Day
Sunny Farm
Summerville
NJ 98765

What do I need?

Here are the basic things you need to become a desktop designer. You may have all of them already, especially if your computer is quite new.

Your computer

This book has been written to be used with a PC (personal computer) which is using the Microsoft® Windows® 95, 98, NT or 2000 operating system. It could be a desktop PC, like the one in the picture, or a smaller laptop or notebook PC.

If you have a different type of computer, such as an Apple Mac, you can still use the design tips and project ideas, and adapt them for your own system. You probably won't be able to follow all our instructions exactly, but most word-processing programs are quite similar. You should be able to use the 'Help' function in your word-processor to work out how to do the same things.

Word-processing software

The projects in the main part of this book use Microsoft® Word 2000. This is a general word-processing program which many people have on their computers. If you don't have Word, you should still be able to do some of the projects using a simpler word-processor such as Microsoft® WordPad, which is included with Windows® 95, 98, NT and 2000.

This is a desktop PC. Your PC may look slightly different, but it should have a main processing unit, a monitor, a keyboard and a mouse.

This computer has an inkjet printer. Inkjets are the cheapest and most common printers available, and are recommended for all the projects in this book.

STARLAB

dance, garage, r&b
featuring dj darren
the cube club
friday 7 november @ 7pm
admission free

Monitor

Processing unit

Mouse mat

Mouse

Keyboard

Other software

If you want to create your own pictures, you'll need an art program such as Paint. Paint comes free with Windows® 95, 98, NT and 2000, and most computers come with some type of art software. You can also use software packages containing pictures and fonts (lettering styles). There's more about these on pages 17 and 18.

Printing

You'll need a printer (an inkjet is best) to turn your finished designs into paper publications. Most printers today can print in colour, but you can get good results using just black and white. If you don't have a printer, you might be able to get your work printed out at a copy shop or a library, at school or at a friend's house.

Some of the projects also require special types of computer printing paper and card. There's more about printers and printing materials on pages 44-45.

You can buy special printer papers, also known as special media, at computer stores.

Blank cards

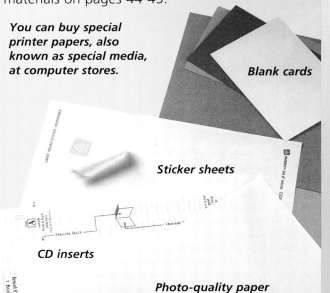

Sticker sheets

CD inserts

Photo-quality paper

Extra stuff

These things will be useful when it comes to finding pictures for your publications...

A scanner
This lets you copy photos, artwork and other pictures into your computer to use in your designs. If you don't have your own, you can pay to use a scanner at a copy shop or library. There is more about scanners on page 45.

An Internet connection
If your computer is connected to the Internet, you'll be able to find lots of extra pictures and fonts (styles of type or lettering) on the World Wide Web. You can often download them and use them for free in your desktop design publications.

To get connected to the Internet, you need a telephone line, a modem, Internet software and an account with an ISP (Internet Service Provider). Your computer shop should be able to help you with this.

A CD-ROM drive
This is also very useful, because software, pictures and fonts often come on CDs. Most PCs come with a built-in CD-ROM drive, but you can also buy them separately.

All about good design

A really good piece of design makes people interested, so they'll want to have a closer look. It also makes information easy to understand, and creates the right "feel" or mood, using a combination of different elements.

Design elements

Design elements are the different things that make a design work. These are the main design elements:

 Lettering Also known as the **font** or **typeface**. By changing the size and style of the lettering, you can change the impact of the text, and make important bits, such as titles, stand out.

Layout Layout is the way the text and pictures are positioned or "laid out" on the paper. Good layout makes the page look balanced, and helps the reader to see everything in the right order.

Colour Designers choose colours that look good together and send the right message. For example, bright, simple colours such as blue, red and yellow are often used in comics and cartoons.

Illustration A big part of a designer's job is choosing the right illustrations, or pictures. The style of the pictures should match the whole design.

Decoration Extra bits of decoration, such as rules, borders, boxes, bars, icons and patterned backgrounds, can add to the mood and make your designs look more professional.

Keep it simple

One of the most important rules of good design is to keep all the elements quite simple. Too many different fonts, colours and pictures can be ugly and confusing. A cluttered, complicated layout could make your publication hard to read.

These two posters show how a designer could present the same information in two different ways.

On this poster, the heading is too small - it would be hard to see from a distance.

The colours clash, making the picture hard to see and the text hard to read.

The important details about when the play is on are lost among the decorations at the bottom.

This title here is in a large font, which makes it stand out better. It has a spooky, old-fashioned feel, suited to the subject.

A simple picture, using just two contrasting colours, helps reinforce the horror theme.

The design process

It takes time to plan a design, try different styles and make decisions about all the elements. So don't worry if it doesn't look right at first. It's best to work through a "design process", like this:

Research Look at the designs used in magazines, TV shows and books to work out how to get the feel you want. In the pages below, from a science fiction magazine, blue colours and computer-style fonts are used to give a space-age feel.

Planning It can help to make small, rough design sketches, called thumbnails, on a piece of paper, to test out different ideas before using your computer.

Setting the style Next, choose the fonts, colours and other elements you're going to use. This is known as "setting the style".

Layout Once you've collected all the elements, you can start arranging them. Designers usually experiment with several different layouts and choose the one they like best.

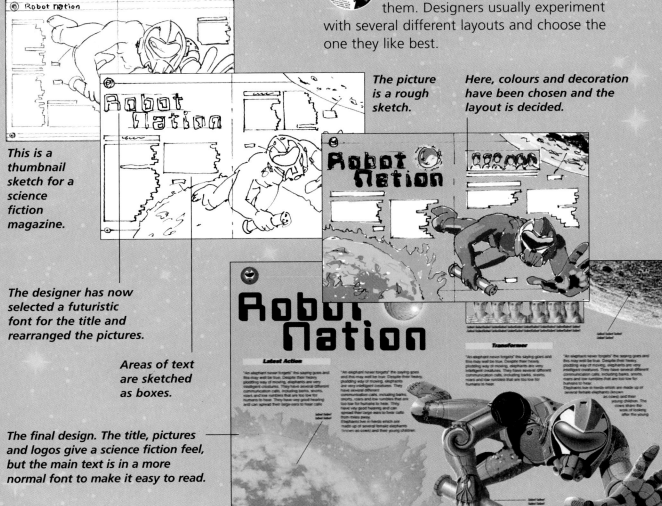

This is a thumbnail sketch for a science fiction magazine.

The designer has now selected a futuristic font for the title and rearranged the pictures.

Areas of text are sketched as boxes.

The final design. The title, pictures and logos give a science fiction feel, but the main text is in a more normal font to make it easy to read.

The picture is a rough sketch.

Here, colours and decoration have been chosen and the layout is decided.

Using Microsoft® Word 2000

The next four pages explain the basics of Microsoft® Word 2000, for those who haven't used it before. You can turn back to these pages if you get stuck while you're doing the projects later on in the book.

What is Word?

Microsoft® Word 2000 is a word-processing program, which means it's usually used for writing letters, essays and other documents. However, it also lets you add pictures and decorations, and do interesting things with text, so it's ideal for desktop publishing projects as well.

Finding and opening Word

Once your PC is switched on, you can open Word. Click on *Start* in the bottom left-hand corner of the screen, then move your mouse pointer over *Programs*. You should see a list of the programs on your computer. If you have Word, it should be there. Click on it to start the program.

(If you have bought Word, but it isn't on your computer yet, follow the instructions that come with it to find out how to load it onto your PC.)

The "paper" you see on the screen corresponds to the shape of the paper you'll print your work out on.

What you see

When you start Word, it automatically opens a new document for you to work in. The document looks like a page of white paper on the screen. If you click on *View* in the menu bar at the top of the screen, you can choose from several different ways of looking at your document. The easiest is probably *Print Layout*, as it shows you exactly how your finished page will appear.

Your screen will look something like this when you've chosen the Print Layout viewing option.

Paper

Setting up your page

First you need to tell Word what size of paper you want to use, and whether you want it to be upright (portrait) or on its side (landscape).

To do this, click on *File* in the menu bar, then click on *Page Setup...* from the drop-down menu. When the *Page Setup* dialog box appears, click on the *Paper Size* tab at the top. You can now choose the paper size. Start with the type of paper you normally use, such as A4 or letter paper. You can also choose whether to make it portrait or landscape.

You choose the paper size here. Click the arrow to see a menu, then click on the paper you want.

You can use these boxes to enter a "custom" paper size ~ one that isn't in the menu.

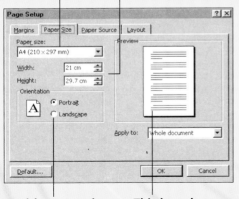

Choose either portrait or landscape here.

This box shows you what your chosen page setup will look like.

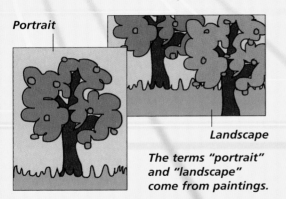

Portrait

Landscape

The terms "portrait" and "landscape" come from paintings.

Setting margins

You may want to change the margins (the gaps around the edge of the paper), especially if your printer leaves large margins when it prints. To do this, click on the *Margins* tab in the *Page Setup* dialog box. It allows you to type in the size of the top, bottom, left and right margins.

Margin measurement

Dominic Duffy
1 Repro Road,
Quadport QX1 AA
d.duffy@coolweb.com
0111 622 054

You fill in the margin sizes you want in these boxes.

The preview box shows how the margins will look.

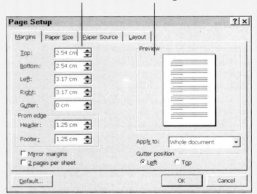

Don't worry about the other options in the Page Setup *dialog box ~ just leave them as they are.*

Ready to write

When you've set your paper size and margins, click on *OK*. The *Page Setup* dialog box will disappear, and you're ready to write. The flashing cursor, which looks like a small vertical line, shows where the text will appear when you start typing. Once you've written some text, you can move the cursor to anywhere in the text to make changes or corrections. To do this, just click on the text with your mouse.

The Word 2000 screen

Word tools

Word's main screen may look complicated, but it makes sense once you know which symbols represent which tools, and what they can do. If you let your cursor rest over a symbol for a moment, a label will appear telling you the name of the tool. If you first select *What's This?* in the *Help* menu, then click on a symbol, a label will appear describing what that tool does.

Missing options

The Word 2000 menu and toolbar are designed to remember which options you use the most. If you haven't used something recently, it may seem to disappear from your screen ~ but don't panic. If you click on a word on the menu bar (*File* for example), you'll see a short list of options. Click on the arrows at the bottom of the list, and the complete menu will reappear. Then just click on any option you want to restore.

When you're using Word, if something doesn't work, it may help simply to try it again. If your computer "crashes" (freezes up), you may need to switch it off and start again.

When you first start up Word, the screen will probably look similar to this. If you can't see all these symbols on your screen, click on View and select Toolbars, then select Formatting, Standard and Drawing from the list.

Spelling and grammar – checks text for mistakes, and suggests corrections

Save – saves the document you are working on

Copy – copies text or an image, which you can then paste somewhere else

New – opens up a new document

Open – opens up an existing document

Print – prints out your document

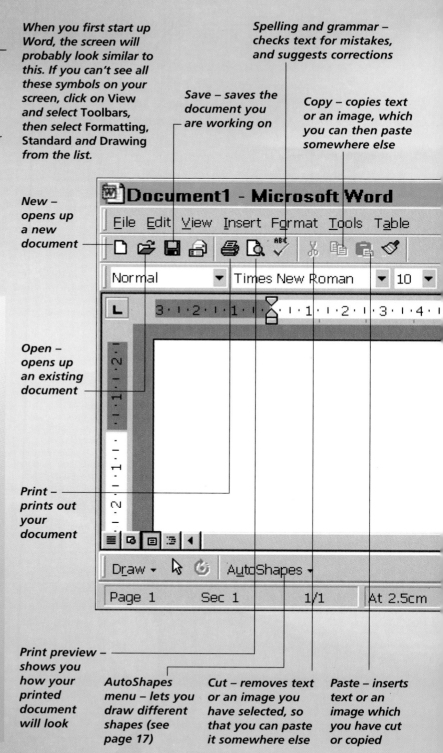

Print preview – shows you how your printed document will look

AutoShapes menu – lets you draw different shapes (see page 17)

Cut – removes text or an image you have selected, so that you can paste it somewhere else

Paste – inserts text or an image which you have cut or copied

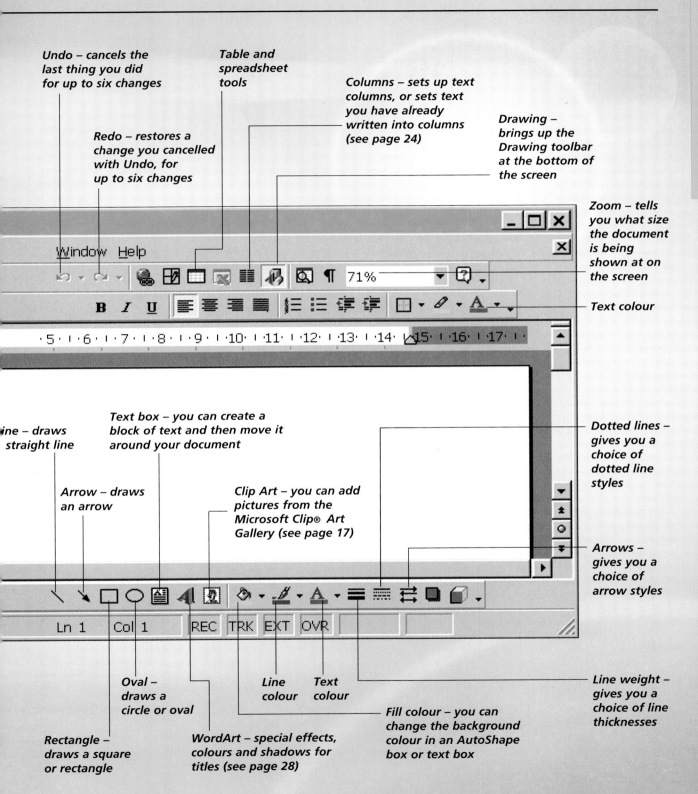

Undo – cancels the last thing you did for up to six changes

Redo – restores a change you cancelled with Undo, for up to six changes

Table and spreadsheet tools

Columns – sets up text columns, or sets text you have already written into columns (see page 24)

Drawing – brings up the Drawing toolbar at the bottom of the screen

Zoom – tells you what size the document is being shown at on the screen

Text colour

Line – draws a straight line

Text box – you can create a block of text and then move it around your document

Arrow – draws an arrow

Clip Art – you can add pictures from the Microsoft Clip® Art Gallery (see page 17)

Dotted lines – gives you a choice of dotted line styles

Arrows – gives you a choice of arrow styles

Rectangle – draws a square or rectangle

Oval – draws a circle or oval

WordArt – special effects, colours and shadows for titles (see page 28)

Line colour

Text colour

Fill colour – you can change the background colour in an AutoShape box or text box

Line weight – gives you a choice of line thicknesses

Start simple

For your first design project, try something simple, such as a letterhead to make all your letters look smart and professional. This project lets you experiment with lettering and layout.

Getting started

Start your Word program and choose the paper size you normally use for letters (probably A4 or letter paper). For a reminder of how to do this, see page 8.

Then type in all the details you want to include, like your name, address, phone number and e-mail address.

Word adds these red and green squiggles to words and sentences it doesn't recognize. You can ignore them for now ~ they won't show on your printout.

*Press the **Return** key to make a line break for each new line.*

Here are some style and layout ideas for your letterhead:

Change the style

To change the style of text, you have to highlight it. Move your mouse pointer to where the text starts, hold down the main (left) mouse button and move the pointer to the end of the text. When the words are highlighted, release the mouse button.

Font list — **Font size list** — **Style buttons** — **Highlighted text**

A rule under the text makes the letterhead look neat.

Try using italic for the details.

Try using small letters or capitals for all the words. What kind of effect does this have?

d.duffy@coolweb.com

Dominic Duffy
1 Repro Road · Quadport QX1 AA · d.duffy@coolweb.com

Dominic Duffy
1 Repro Road,
Quadport QX1 AA
d.duffy@coolweb.com

dominic duffy
1 repro road
quadport
qx1 aa

d.duffy@coolweb.com

• To change the lettering, or font, click on the arrow in the font list, which is a small box near the top left of the screen (shown in the picture opposite). A list of fonts will appear. Select one of them, and your highlighted text will change to that font. (You may not have many fonts just yet, but you can find out how to get more on pages 18-19).

• To change the size, click on the font size list next to the font list. Font size is measured in points (one point is 1/72inch or 0.035mm). 12 or 14 points is a good size to start with.

• To make text **bold**, *italic* or <u>underlined</u>, highlight it and click on one of the style buttons. To undo a style, click again on the same button. When you've finished, click somewhere else in the document to undo the highlighting.

Change the layout

There are lots of ways to change the layout of your letterhead to make it more interesting. Here are just a few.

• Use the *Return* key to insert extra spaces between lines.

Return key

• You could put all your details onto one long line. Use the *Delete* key to undo any line breaks and line spaces you've put in.

Delete key

• To add a rule right across the page under your details, type three minus signs, then press *Return*. Use three equals signs in the same way for a double rule.

Minus key   **Equals key**

• To change the alignment (the way the text lines up), highlight the text and click on one of these buttons, which appear in the toolbar at the top of the screen.

This button aligns text along the left of the page, like this.

This button centres text in the middle, like this.

This button aligns text along the right of the page, like this.

Print it

When you're happy with your letterhead, save it and print it out. For extra help with printing, see page 44.

You can either type out your letter, or print out the letterhead and then write your message by hand.

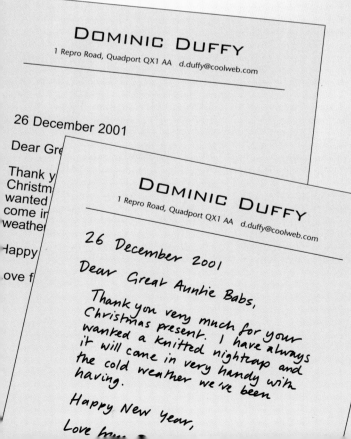

DOMINIC DUFFY

1 Repro Road, Quadport QX1 AA   d.duffy@coolweb.com

26 December 2001

Dear Gr

Thank y
Christm
wanted
come ir
weathe

Happy

ove f

DOMINIC DUFFY

1 Repro Road, Quadport QX1 AA   d.duffy@coolweb.com

26 December 2001

Dear Great Auntie Babs,

Thank you very much for your Christmas present. I have always wanted a knitted nightcap and it will come in very handy with the cold weather we've been having.

Happy New Year,

Love fr

Creating pictures

Most of the projects in the book include pictures as well as words. The next four pages show you how to create and collect pictures that can be used on a computer, and how to put them into your desktop designs.

Digital pictures

The simplest way to add pictures to your designs is to draw or paint them onto the paper after printing out the words. This works well if you're good at drawing. However, using digital (computerized) pictures in your designs gives you much more choice and control. You can move pictures around on the screen, and try different effects and layouts before printing out your final design.

If you want to add artwork by hand, leave a space in your document before printing it out.

Creating pictures with Paint

Microsoft® Paint is a painting and drawing program that comes with Windows® 95, 98, NT and 2000. You'll find it under *Accessories* in the *Programs* menu. You can use it to make digital pictures, which you can then save and use in your Word designs (see the next page for how to do this).

The Paint screen has a drawing area and a selection of tools and colours which you select with the mouse.

Design tips

When you're using Paint, you don't have to try to make your pictures look like real-life painted pictures. Instead, experiment with the Paint tools to make bright, bold images.

The Tiger

A tiger prowled through the
Hiding his striking stripes in
He heard a wild boar browsin
And stood stone-still, sniffing
He crouched down low and cre
Then leaped, a lightning flash of

Printing your document on coloured paper makes it more eye-catching.

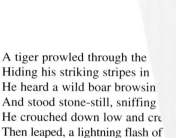

The Tiger

A tiger prowled through the thick forest,
Hiding his striking stripes in the green grass.
He heard a wild boar browsing in the bushes
And stood stone-still, sniffing the scent,
He crouched down low and crept up slowly,
Then leaped, a lightning flash of orange and black.

This is the Paint screen. The fish has been drawn using the Brush, Circle, Fill and Spray tools.

Use the Help option from the menu bar to find out all the things you can do with Paint.

The white area is the "paper".

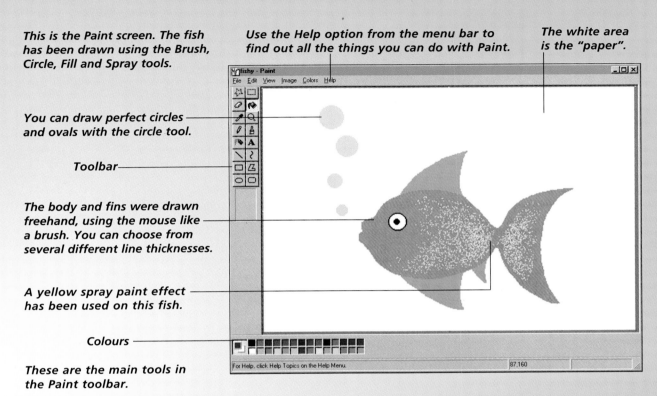

You can draw perfect circles and ovals with the circle tool.

Toolbar

The body and fins were drawn freehand, using the mouse like a brush. You can choose from several different line thicknesses.

A yellow spray paint effect has been used on this fish.

Colours

These are the main tools in the Paint toolbar.

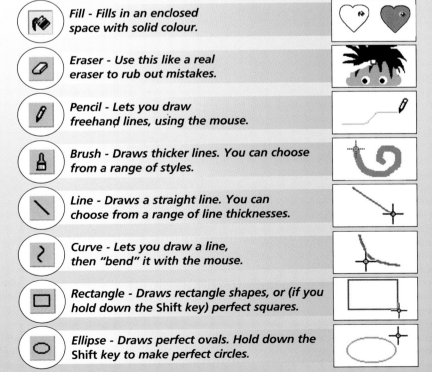

Fill - *Fills in an enclosed space with solid colour.*

Eraser - *Use this like a real eraser to rub out mistakes.*

Pencil - *Lets you draw freehand lines, using the mouse.*

Brush - *Draws thicker lines. You can choose from a range of styles.*

Line - *Draws a straight line. You can choose from a range of line thicknesses.*

Curve - *Lets you draw a line, then "bend" it with the mouse.*

Rectangle - *Draws rectangle shapes, or (if you hold down the Shift key) perfect squares.*

Ellipse - *Draws perfect ovals. Hold down the Shift key to make perfect circles.*

Saving picture files

When your picture is finished, click on *File* and *Save*. Paint will let you name the file and will automatically save it with the ending .bmp, short for "bitmap". For example, the picture above is called "fishy.bmp". A bitmap is a type of picture file which can be used in Word documents.

It's a good idea to make a special folder on your computer to store all your pictures in. Then, when you want to use them in your design documents, they'll be easy to find.

Adding pictures

This page explains how to put a .bmp picture file, such as a Paint file, into a Word document. The opposite page shows you some other ways of finding and creating pictures to use in your designs.

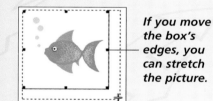

Highlight the right picture file here.

The picture is shown in this box.

Click on Insert to put the picture into your Word document.

Adding a picture

To add a Paint picture to a Word document:

• Click on *Insert* in the menu bar. Click on *Picture*, and then select *From File...* from the menu that appears.

• A directory of the folders on your computer will appear. Find the folder where you stored your picture, and highlight the file.

• Click on *Insert*. The picture will appear in your Word document. If you click on it, you'll see that it is in a box. You can drag the picture with your mouse to move it around, or make it bigger or smaller by clicking and dragging the box's corners.

If you move the box's edges, you can stretch the picture.

Cropping the picture box

Once you've inserted a picture, the picture toolbar shown here should appear somewhere on your screen. (If it doesn't, click on *View* and select *Toolbars*, then *Picture*.) If you click on the *Crop* tool, moving the corners of the picture box makes the box smaller, without changing the size of picture.

Crop tool

This way, you can make sure the picture box doesn't take up too much space on the page.

Add text

If you click away from the picture, you'll be able to write text as normal. For example, you could make a letterhead like the ones on page 12, and decorate it with a picture.

Marina Fish • 14 Seaview Street •
marina@webnet.com

Dawn Day
Sunny Far
Summervi

AutoShapes

Word can draw a selection of shapes for you. To do this, click on *View* in the menu bar. Select *Toolbars*, then *Drawing*. The drawing toolbar will appear near the bottom of the screen. Click on *AutoShapes*.

You can now choose from several groups of shapes. Try *Basic Shapes* to start with, and click on a shape you like.

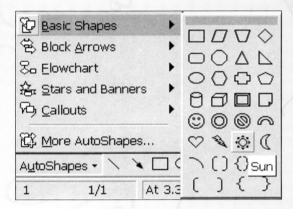

Now click and drag with the mouse to draw the shape on your page. If you hold down the *Shift* key, it will stay the same shape. If you don't press the *Shift* key, you can stretch the shape. You can also move the shape by clicking on it and dragging it with your mouse.

You can still change the shape after you've drawn it, by moving the corners.

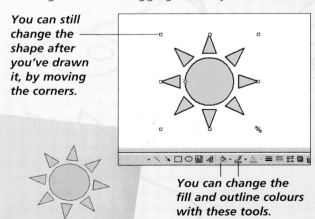

You can change the fill and outline colours with these tools.

Clip Art

Clip Art is a name for picture files that anyone can use in their designs. There are several ways to get Clip Art pictures:

Clip Art button

Microsoft® Clip Gallery
This selection of pictures comes with Word. Click on *Insert* in the menu bar, select *Picture* and *Clip Art...* or click on the *Clip Art* button (above) on your drawing tool bar, if you can see it. You'll see a box of Clip Art pictures organized into topics. When you find one you like, right click on it and select *Insert*. The picture will appear in your document.

A Clip Art picture of a tortoise from the Microsoft® Clip Gallery

On the Web
Lots of Web sites provide free Clip Art (see page 47). To copy a picture from the Web, click on it with the right mouse button. Select *Save Picture As...* from the menu that appears, name the picture and choose the option that lets you save it as a bitmap (.bmp) file. You can then store it on your computer and copy it into Word.

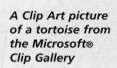

A picture of cherries from the www. clipartconnection .com Web site

CD-ROMs
You can buy CD-ROMs full of Clip Art pictures on all kinds of subjects, such as sports or science. Look out for them at your computer store.

Fonts

A font is a set of letters, numbers and other characters in a particular style. Choosing the best fonts for your designs helps you create the right mood and get your message across.

Types of fonts

There are thousands of fonts, divided into several main groups. Each font has its own name.

• **Serif fonts** have small tabs or serifs on each letter. They make good body fonts, because the serifs help your eye move along lines of text.

serif

This traditional-looking serif font is called Garamond.

• **Sanserif or "sans" fonts** don't have serifs. They look clean and modern.

This popular sanserif font is called Gill Sans.

• **Body fonts** are easy to read and usually have serifs. They are used for long passages of text.

This body font is called Times.

 *GhoulyCaps*

 WantedPoster

 *OldEnglish*

• **Display fonts** are eyecatching with a strong "mood". They're ideal for large poster titles, or for stickers or badges.

• **Dingbats** are fonts made up of little pictures instead of letters.

Webdings

Changing fonts in Word

When you're using Word, you can change any character, word or chunk of text into a different font. Just click and drag the mouse to highlight the bit of text you want to change, then choose a font from the font list near the top left of the screen. You can also change the size of the font, using the font size list.

Font list   **Font size list**

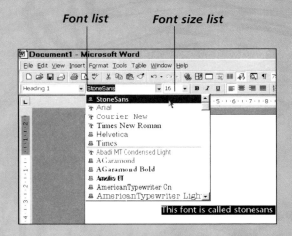

Get new fonts

Word comes with a few fonts, but what if you need more? Just like Clip Art pictures, you can buy large collections of fonts quite cheaply on CD-ROMs at your computer store. You can also download free fonts from the Web. Some good free font Web sites are listed on page 47.

Start designing

You only need a few fonts to create eyecatching posters, flyers and leaflets. The example opposite shows some of the design tricks you could try.

Poster planning

First, work out what your poster needs to say and try out a few small sketches. Start a new Word file, select A4 or letter paper (see page 9), and type in all the text. Then you can start to experiment with different fonts and layouts.

The image on a poster should be bold and simple. You can use a Clip Art picture (see page 17), but posters can also look effective if you use a shape from Word's *AutoShapes* menu, or even a picture from a picture font.

Design tips

Don't use lots of fonts in the same design ~ it will look confusing. Stick to just one or two.

The title on this poster is in a futuristic font called Amoebia.

The star in this version of the poster is from the Dingbats1 font.

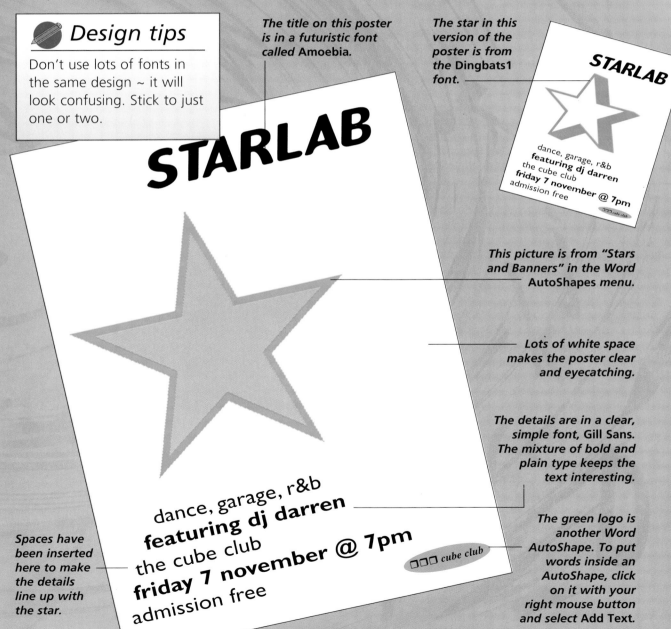

This picture is from "Stars and Banners" in the Word AutoShapes menu.

Lots of white space makes the poster clear and eyecatching.

The details are in a clear, simple font, Gill Sans. The mixture of bold and plain type keeps the text interesting.

The green logo is another Word AutoShape. To put words inside an AutoShape, click on it with your right mouse button and select Add Text.

Spaces have been inserted here to make the details line up with the star.

Colours

Like fonts, colours can have all kinds of different effects. This page explains how to use colour in your designs.

Colour combinations

It's a good idea not to use too many colours at once. The best book covers, logos and posters are often made up of just two or three colours which go together really well. You'll need to experiment with different colour combinations for each project, but here are some suggestions:

Orange/blue, red/green and purple/yellow are contrasting combinations. They have a bright, jumpy effect.

Lime green with another bright colour has a very modern, funky feel.

Black and red together look bold and dramatic.

You can also get a striking effect by mixing black with another bright colour such as orange or yellow.

If you combine lively colours such as red, bright pink and orange, you'll get a vibrant, dizzying effect ~ the colours will seem to vibrate when you look at them.

Two similar colours such as blue and green, or two shades of the same colour, have a calming, slightly old-fashioned feel.

It's a wrap...

When designers need some wrapping paper, they just make their own on the computer.

To do this, start a new A4 or letter-paper size Word document, and simply arrange coloured AutoShapes, Paint pictures or picture font pictures (see pages 14-17) all over it.

You can repeat the same picture or AutoShape by duplicating it. Move your mouse pointer over the shape until you see a four-way arrow, then click to select the shape. Then hold down the *Control* key and press *D* (for "duplicate"). A copy of the shape will appear, and you can move it to where you want it using the mouse.

When it's ready, print out a few sheets of your wrapping paper in colour, and tape them together until you have a piece big enough to wrap your present.

The moons and stars, circles, rockets and diamonds on these designs are made up of different Word AutoShapes.

Personal paper

If you're making wrapping paper for a particular person, why not put their name on

Happy Birthday Becky

it? The easiest way is to draw a large AutoShape, then click on it with your right mouse button and select *Add Text*. You can then write the person's name or a birthday message inside the shape.

The flower design below was drawn in Paint, then inserted into a Word document.

Computer colours

Paint and Word give you a wide choice of colours. Paint also lets you create new ones:

• **Paint** Paint has a palette of colours at the bottom of the screen. To make a new one, click on *Colors* in the menu bar (in some versions, you'll find *Colors* under *Options*). Select *Edit Colors...* In the box that appears, click on *Define Custom Colors*. Choose a new colour and add it to the palette by clicking on *Add to Custom Colors*.

Use the mouse to select a colour here.

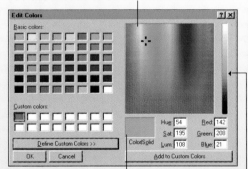

The colour you've picked will show here.

Move this marker to select the right shade.

• **Word 2000** To change the text colour, highlight the text and click on the arrow by the *Font Color* button at the bottom of the screen. You'll see a choice of colours ~ click on one and the text will change. If you click on *More Colors...*, you'll see an even wider range of colours.

Font Color button

For AutoShapes, move the pointer over the shape until you see a four-way arrow. Click to select the shape, then click on the arrows next to the *Fill Color* and *Line Color* buttons to see a choice of colours.

Fill Color button

Line Color button

Sizes and shapes

You don't have to stick to A4 or letter paper for your desktop designs. Word can create documents in many other sizes, from postcards to bookmarks.

Special media

Things like postcards and invitations work best if you print them on special "media", such as card or stiff paper. You'll have to adjust your printer for special media ~ check with the printer manual. You'll also have to move the printer's guides to keep smaller media in place. (For some useful printing tips, see page 44.)

You can buy plain blank postcards from stationery stores.

Art stores often sell individual sheets of card in different colours and textures, which you can cut to any size and shape.

If you use dark card, dark or bright colours will look best on the printout.

These pictures were done in Paint and inserted into Word (see page 16). For the words, add a text box on top (see page 29).

Make a postcard

If your card is an unusual size, measure it along both edges and write down the measurements. Then start a new Word document (see page 8), and in the *Page Setup* box, type the size of your card into the *Width and Height* boxes.

Paper Size *tab*   **Type the measurements in here.**

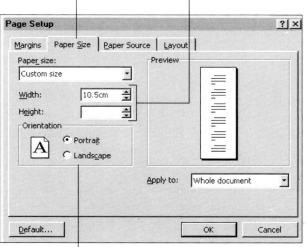

Choose Portrait or Landscape here.

Set the margins as small as you can (Word will correct them if you make them too small.) Now you're ready to design and print your postcard. Like posters, postcards look best with a simple picture and message.

Invitations

Postcard-sized cards make good invitations. Or, if you want to make a lot, you can do several invitations on one bigger piece of card, and cut them up afterwards.

To do this, start a new Word document and set the paper size to the same size as your card (such as A4).

Next, draw a table. To do this:

• Click on *Table* in the menu bar. Select *Insert Table...* This dialog box will appear:
• Fill in the boxes as shown above. (It's best to have just a few columns and rows so your invitations aren't too small.) Click on *OK*.
• You'll now see a table on your page.

Insert Table ? X
Table size
Number of columns: 5
Number of rows: 2
AutoFit behavior
◉ Fixed column width: Auto
○ AutoFit to contents
○ AutoFit to window
Table format (none) AutoFormat...
☐ Set as default for new tables
OK Cancel

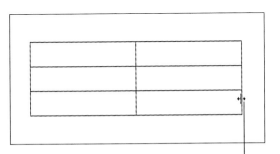

You can make the table wider by clicking and dragging the lines with your mouse.

Multiple copies

Type the text of your invitation into the first box ~ the box will get bigger as you write. Now design the layout. Try using different fonts, adding pictures, or putting text in AutoShapes. Press the *Return* key if you need to add space.

When it's done, copy it into the other boxes. To copy text, highlight it and press the *Control* key and the *C* key. Then move the cursor to the next box and press *Control* and *V*. To copy an AutoShape or picture, move your mouse over it until you see a four-way arrow, then click to select it. Then copy it using *Control + C* and *Control + V* again.

This is an AutoShape with text inside (see page 19).

When you've printed out the page, cut out each invitation along the lines with a craft knife or scissors.

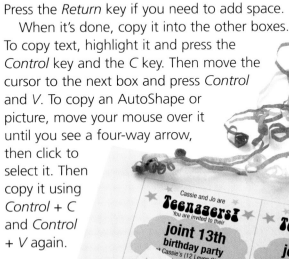

Folding documents

When you're making a folding card or leaflet, you have to know where to put the design on the page so that it looks right after it's printed out and folded.

Plan the layout

To make a simple greetings card you'll need a piece of thin or medium card. Make a new Word document the same size as your whole piece of card, using the *Page Setup* box (see page 22). To make a portrait-shaped card like the ones here, select "Landscape" in the *Paper Size* menu and set the margins as small as you can. Now select *Print Layout* in the *View* menu and click on *Zoom* followed by *Whole Page*.

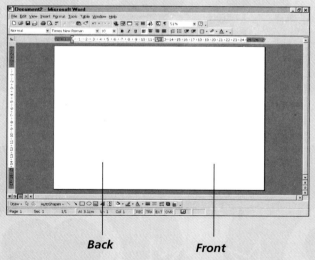

Back **Front**

Your document should look like this. The right-hand half of the page will become the front of the card, and the left-hand half will become the back, as shown here. To divide the page in half, click on *Format* in the menu bar, select *Columns...* from the drop-down menu, then choose *Two*. Press the *Return* key to insert spaces in your document until the cursor appears at the top of the right-hand side. Now you're ready to design the front of your card.

Adding words

If you want to add a message, such as "Merry Christmas" or "Congratulations!", make a text box by clicking on *Insert* in the menu bar and selecting *Text Box*. Then type the text in the box. Now you can move the text around and position it where you want it.

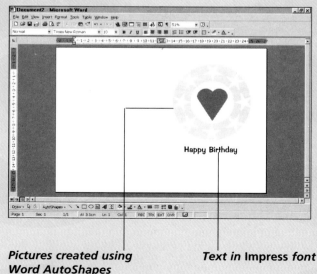

Pictures created using Word AutoShapes

Text in Impress font

Remember that when you print, your printer will leave a margin around the edge of the card.

Good Luck!

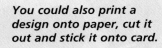

You could also print a design onto paper, cut it out and stick it onto card.

Print it out

When you print out your card, remember to set your printer to the right size and thickness for the paper or card you are using (see page 44). Then gently score a line down the middle using a ruler and a blunt knife or a pen that has run out of ink. You can then fold the card neatly.

A message inside

You can just write inside your card with a pen. But if you want to use Word to add more text or pictures to the inside of the card, simply make another Word file just like the first one. Again, write the main message on the right-hand side. Then print this document out on the other side of your card before you fold it in half.

More folding

You can make three-way folding cards and leaflets by choosing three columns instead of two. This diagram shows one way to fold them.

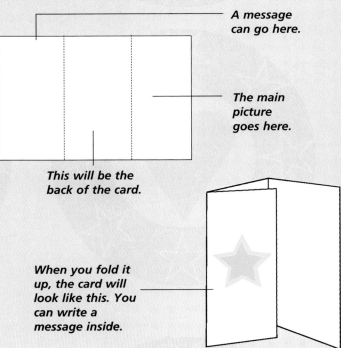

A message can go here.

The main picture goes here.

This will be the back of the card.

When you fold it up, the card will look like this. You can write a message inside.

Sticker sheets

Want to make your own cool stickers? You can buy sticker sheets in computer stores and stationers, full of blank stickers waiting for your designs.

Measure your sheets

First of all, measure your sticker sheet. Write down how big the stickers are and how far each one is from the top and left-hand side of the sheet.

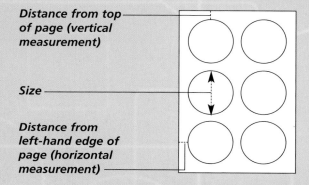

Distance from top of page (vertical measurement)

Size

Distance from left-hand edge of page (horizontal measurement)

Create a sticker document

In Word, start a new document. Set the paper size to the same size as the sticker sheet. Then use Word AutoShapes to draw each sticker in roughly the right place on the page. For example, if your sheet has six round stickers, draw six round AutoShapes as guide shapes.

Now click on the first shape with your right mouse button, and select *Format AutoShape* from the menu that appears. Under the *Size* tab, enter the size of your sticker.

Next, click on the *Layout* tab followed by *Advanced*. You'll see a box like the one shown on the right. Enter the distance of the first sticker from the top and left-hand side of the page. When you click on *OK*, the guide shape will be exactly the right size and in the right place. Repeat this for all the stickers.

Sticker suggestions

Now you can put your designs in the sticker shapes. Here are some ideas...

 Pictures A sticker can be just a picture. Design your own using Paint (see page 14) or use Clip Art or Word AutoShapes (see page 17) to make bright, bold stickers.

Words You can put words in a sticker shape, or in any other Word AutoShape, by right-clicking on it and selecting *Add Text*. Stickers also look good with WordArt (see Text Effects on page 28).

Colours Use the AutoShapes tools to change the colours of text, background and AutoShapes. Click on your shape or highlight your text, then select one of these tools:

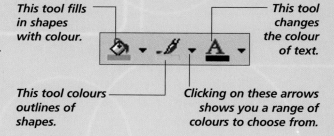

This tool fills in shapes with colour.

This tool changes the colour of text.

This tool colours outlines of shapes.

Clicking on these arrows shows you a range of colours to choose from.

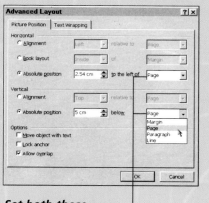

Set both these boxes to "Page".

This is an AutoShape with text inside.

Leave a space, just in case

Even if you position the shapes carefully, your printer might not be able to print them in exactly the right place. Make sure you allow for this in your designs.

If you want a sticker with a white background, like this, leave some space all around your design.

White space

On the other hand, if you want to fill the sticker with colour, make your background shape bigger than the sticker really is, to make sure it's all covered. Professional designers call this a bleed.

Edge of real sticker

Bleed

Remove the guides

When you've finished, if you can still see your guide shapes, click on them and change their outline colour to "No Line", so you can't see them and they won't show on your stickers. Then, you can set up your printer (see page 44) and print out your stickers.

Badges and buttons

Badges and buttons work just like stickers. You get a sheet of shapes, usually circles. But instead of being sticky, they're made of cardboard. They come with plastic parts which you fit together to make your badge or button.

Some stickers just have a message on them.

This shark picture is from the Microsoft® Clip Gallery (see page 17).

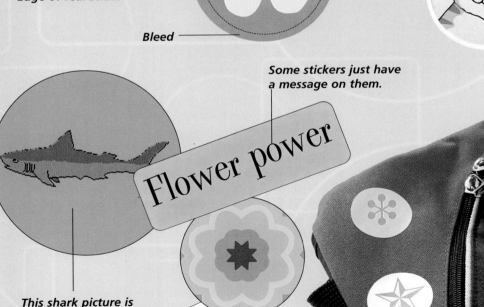

Text effects

Word will let you do all kinds of different things with text to make it look interesting. You can have coloured text, shadows, outlines and special effects, and you can even curve text around pictures.

Styles and colours

To try out some text styles, open a new Word document, write a word, and highlight it with your cursor. Then click on *Format* in the menu bar, and select *Font....* You'll see a box with lots of options.

You can change the font and font size here.

Use this menu to change the colour of text.

These buttons change the text style.

This is what some of the styles look like.

WordArt

Word Art is a facility for making text effects. It's great for exciting headings, posters and stickers.

To use WordArt, click on *Insert* in the menu bar, select *Picture*, and choose *WordArt....* You'll see a selection of WordArt styles. When you pick one, a box will appear where you can write your text and select the font and font size. (A single word or short phrase works best.) Click on *OK* and your WordArt will appear in your document.

You can drag your WordArt around and change its size, just like a picture. The *WordArt* toolbar automatically appears and you can use it to change the colour and shape of your WordArt.

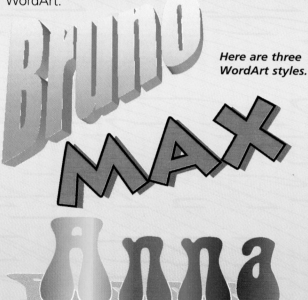

Here are three WordArt styles.

✏️ Design tips

Remember to save amazing text effects like these for big, bold headings. If you use them for long passages of small text, you could make it hard to read.

Text wrapping

Making text fit around a picture is called wrapping. To do it, click on the picture with your right mouse button and select *Format Picture*.

Then select the *Layout* tab, which will give you a choice of several ways of wrapping the text. For example, *Square* leaves a square space around the picture. *Tight* wraps the text closely around the picture.

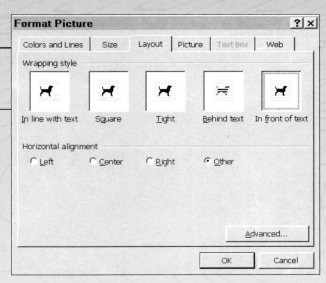

This dialog box lets you choose a wrapping style.

INTRODUCTION

Hippos are among the largest land mammals in the world. They live in and around rivers in Africa and are very good swimmers. They are herbivores and eat mostly grass and a few underwater plants.

HIPPO ANATOMY

Hippos are huge. A fully grown male hippo can be up to 5m (16 ft) long and weigh up to 3,630 kilos (8,000 pounds). Even though they look fat and clumsy, Hippos are very strong and can run as fast as a human being.

Eyes
Ears
Nostrils

A hippois eyes, ears and nostrils are on top of its head so that they stick out of the water.

A HIPPO'S DAY

Hippos spend most of the day underwater, where they can stay cool. In the evenings, they come out of the water and spend several hours eating grass at their feeding grounds.

Text boxes

You can put a piece of text in its own box, so you can move it around just like a picture. To do this, click on *Insert* in the menu bar, wait until the full list of options appears, then select *Text Box*. Now you can type in your text.

Here's a one-page project on hippos, which was designed using several text effects.

The title was made using WordArt.

The labels are in their own text boxes.

The Autoshapes menu has an option for drawing straight lines.

The headings are in capital letters in an outline style.

The picture at the bottom has a tight text wrap. (After choosing the wrap, you may need to move the picture slightly to make the wrap look right.)

Make a newsletter

Word is ideal for creating newsletters, or illustrated projects. You can arrange text in columns, blocks or boxes, and put pictures wherever you like. Here's how to make a one-page newsletter for your club, school or family.

Plan your publication

First of all, collect all the items you want to include and make a list so you don't leave anything off. If you want to use any pictures, make sure they are saved in digital form (see page 14).

> **Edwards family newsletter**
>
> **Editor's letter**
> **Article about American visit**
> **Announcement - Bob & Becky's triplets**
> **Photo of triplets**
> **Announcement - George's birthday**
> **Recipe**

Then choose your fonts (see page 18). You'll need a serif or clear sanserif font for the main text, and an eyecatching font for the title.

Finally, set up a new Word document with a normal paper size, such as A4 or letter paper.

Make a masthead

Newspapers and newsletters have an area at the top called a masthead, which contains the title of the publication and sometimes a logo as well. It always looks the same so that the publication is easy to recognize. The masthead should be quite big and should run right across the top of the newsletter.

Columns

A typical newsletter is arranged in columns. When you've done the masthead, position the cursor just below it. Click on *Format* in the menu bar, select *Columns...*, and choose three columns.

Select the number of columns here.

"Line between" puts a rule between the columns.

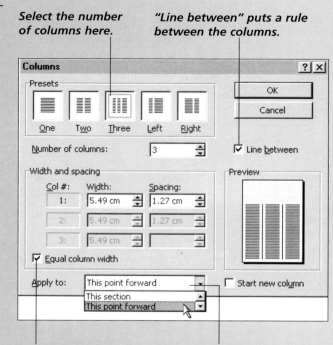

Select "Equal column width" here.

Select "This point forward" in this box, so that the columns do not affect your masthead.

This masthead is decorated with two Word AutoShapes.

This masthead has been made by putting text inside an AutoShape.

Here's a finished newsletter full of family news.

Masthead

The main text of this newsletter is in 12-point Stone Sans font.

The picture caption uses a smaller version of the same font.

The subheadings use the same font, but in bold and slightly larger.

The box about the birthday party takes up two column widths.

The Edwards family newsletter

March 2001

Editor's letter

Welcome to the first edition of the Edwards family newsletter! There are so many members of the Edwards family that I've decided to write this newsletter to help us all keep in touch. If anyone has any announcements they'd like me to put in the newsletter, just email me at josh.edwards@coolweb.com. Or write to me at 12 Techno Terrace, Quadport QU8 1SA, England, UK.

Happy reading...

Josh

American visit

Several members of the American branch of the family visited the UK recently. Uncle Norman's daughter Maggie, her husband Elmer and their children Dexter and Paige came over on holiday from Ipswich, Massachusetts. They stayed with Magenta Edwards in London, where they visited the Tower of London, spent a day at Legoland, and had a ride on the London Eye. They also went to Scotland to see if they could spot the Loch Ness Monster, but came back with a haggis instead.

Bridget, Britney and Blodwen at 2 days old

Bob and Becky's big baby bonanza

On February 12, Bob Edwards and his wife Becky were blessed with not one, not two, but three new little girls! Everything went well and the triplets were born just after midnight. The bouncing babes have been named Bridget, Britney and Blodwen.

Roisina's recipe

Every month the newsletter will contain a recipe, top tip or handy hint from a family member. We're kicking off with my sister Roisina's recipe for roast parsnips.

Method

Cut 500g/1lb parsnips into chip-sized pieces. Spread them out on a non-stick baking tray. Drizzle them with olive oil and sprinkle with salt. Preheat the oven to its hottest setting and roast the parsnips for about 40 minutes, or until crispy and cooked through.

Next month: Uncle Bert shows how to make and decorate your own chocolate eggs for Easter.

Grandpa George turns 100!

After a century of studying sea creatures, fighting in World Wars and drinking a lot of tea, Grandpa George will celebrate his 100th birthday on Thursday 5 April.

Don't miss the party!

A birthday garden party will be held at George's house in Birmingham on Saturday 7 April. All Edwards family members are invited.

The party is being organized by Millie Edwards, George's great niece. E-mail Millie at MillieE@usborne.co.uk, or phone her on 098 765 4321, for all the details.

Design your layout

When you type in your text, Word will automatically run it into the three columns. If you add a picture, give it a text wrap (see page 29) so that the text will run around it. Try to make each text item fit into a column, not run between columns.

Boxes

For a special feature to grab the reader's attention, use a box. Click on *Insert*, select *Text Box* and draw a box using the mouse. Give it a square text wrap (see page 29) and type your text inside.

Four-page booklets

You can make a basic 4-page document from a single piece of paper folded in half. Booklets like this are often used for leaflets, menus and show programmes.

Plan the layout

Just like a folded card, a folded booklet has to be planned to make sure it will look right. An easy way to do this is to take a blank sheet of paper, fold it in half, make notes about what will go where, and then unfold it again. A plan for a pantomime programme is shown here.

Setting up

Start a new Word document as usual, and set it to the right paper size (probably A4 or letter paper) in a landscape layout. Then click on *Format*, select *Columns...*, and choose two columns in the box that appears.

Laying out the pages

In the first column, on the left-hand half of the paper, design the back page of your booklet. In our programme, this is made up of several text boxes (see page 29) containing advertisements. Press the *Return* key several times to move to the next column. (If any of your pictures or boxes move, move them back with the mouse.) Put the front cover in the second column. Like a poster, it should be simple with a large title and maybe a picture. At the end of the page, press the *Return* key again to move to the next page of the document, which will form the two inside pages of the booklet. As before, lay out the text for these two pages in the two columns ~ one column for each page of the booklet.

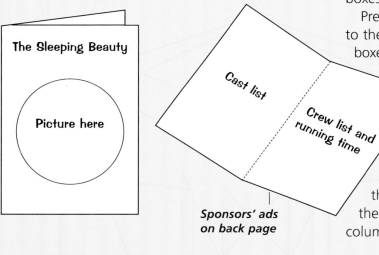

Sponsors' ads on back page

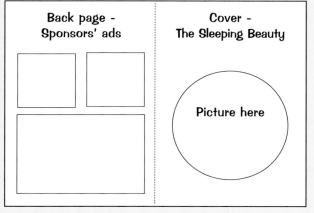

This is how the first page of the document will be laid out, to be printed on one side of the paper.

The second page of the document will be laid out like this, and printed on the other side of the paper.

Lists, tabs and bullets

Booklets often contain lists of information, such as a cast list. Tabs are very useful for lists. When you press the *Tab* key, it creates a space (called an indent) before the next word you type. The *Tab* key is at the top left of the keyboard and has two arrows on it.

Here's an example, showing how to use the *Tab* key to make a list of cast members:

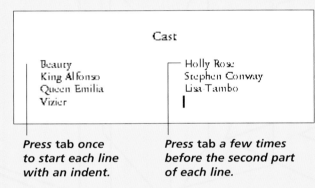

Cast

Beauty   Holly Rose
King Alfonso   Stephen Conway
Queen Emilia   Lisa Tambo
Vizier

Press tab once to start each line with an indent.

Press tab a few times before the second part of each line.

You can also add bullet points to a list. Just highlight the list, click on *Format* in the menu bar, and select *Bullets and Numbering...* You can then choose from a range of different bullet point styles.

Printing booklets

To make the booklet work, you'll have to print it out on both sides of the same sheet of paper. To do this, tell your printer to print just page 1 of the document (see page 44 for printing tips). Then turn the paper over and start printing again, this time telling the printer to print just page 2. (Remember you'll need to make sure the printout is the same way up on both sides.) Finally, carefully fold the paper in half to make the finished booklet.

Design tips

When you're printing on both sides of the paper, it's best to use extra-thick or high-quality paper or thin card, so that the print doesn't show through.

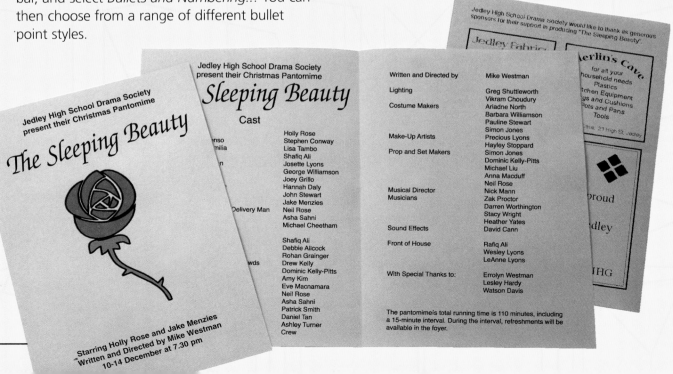

Jedley High School Drama Society present their Christmas Pantomime

The Sleeping Beauty

Starring Holly Rose and Jake Menzies
Written and Directed by Mike Westman
10-14 December at 7.30 pm

Jedley High School Drama Society present their Christmas Pantomime

Sleeping Beauty

Cast

onso	Holly Rose
milia	Stephen Conway
n	Lisa Tambo
	Shafiq Ali
	Josette Lyons
	George Williamson
	Joey Grillo
	Hannah Daly
	John Stewart
	Jake Menzies
Delivery Man	Neil Rose
	Asha Sahni
	Michael Cheetham
	Shafiq Ali
	Debbie Allcock
	Rohan Grainger
	Drew Kelly
wds	Dominic Kelly-Pitts
	Amy Kim
	Eve Macnamara
	Neil Rose
	Asha Sahni
	Patrick Smith
	Daniel Tan
	Ashley Turner
	Crew

Written and Directed by	Mike Westman
Lighting	Greg Shuttleworth
	Vikram Choudury
Costume Makers	Ariadne North
	Barbara Williamson
	Pauline Stewart
	Simon Jones
Make-Up Artists	Precious Lyons
	Hayley Stoppard
Prop and Set Makers	Simon Jones
	Dominic Kelly-Pitts
	Michael Liu
	Anna Macduff
	Neil Rose
Musical Director	Nick Mann
Musicians	Zak Proctor
	Darren Worthington
	Stacy Wright
	Heather Yates
Sound Effects	David Cann
Front of House	Rafiq Ali
	Wesley Lyons
	LeAnne Lyons
With Special Thanks to:	Errolyn Westman
	Lesley Hardy
	Watson Davis

The pantomime is total running time is 110 minutes, including a 15-minute interval. During the interval, refreshments will be available in the foyer.

Jedley High School Drama Society would like to thank its generous sponsors for their support in producing "The Sleeping Beauty".

Jedley Fabrics

Merlin's Cave
for all your household needs
Plastics
Kitchen Equipment
Rugs and Cushions
Pots and Pans
Tools

Cave, 21 High St, Jedley

proud
dley
IHG

Lots of pages

Once you can make a four-page booklet, it's easy to make a whole book by joining several booklets together.

Plan your book

Books are made by folding pieces of paper. This means that, as with the booklet on page 32, you have to put the pages in a particular order in your Word document, to make them appear in the right order when the paper is folded and the pages are put together.

To work out the order, make a blank book first. (Designers call this a dummy.) Take a sheet of paper and fold it in half to make the cover. Then add more folded sheets of paper inside the first one. Each extra sheet of paper will add four pages to your book.

This blank book is made up of three folded pieces of paper. One makes the cover and the other two together make eight pages.

When you have as many pages as you want, hold the sheets of paper together at the fold and write in the page numbers or what you want to go on each page. Then open out the paper. You'll now be able to see how to arrange the pages in your Word document.

Setting up in Word

Start a new Word document and set the right paper size in a landscape layout. Set up two columns, as for a booklet, by selecting *Format* and *Columns...* and clicking on *Two*. Put quite a large gap between the columns, using the "Spacing" box, to make sure no text disappears into the fold, or gutter, of your book. A spacing of about 4cm works well for A4 or letter paper.

You can now write the pages of your book, using your dummy book as a guide to what order to put them in.

This is how the pages would be arranged in a Word document to make the book shown on the left. These Word pages would then be printed out on both sides of three sheets of paper.

Page 1 (front of sheet 1)		Page 2 (back of sheet 1)	
Back cover	Front cover	Inside front cover	Inside back cover

Page 3 (front of sheet 2)		Page 4 (back of sheet 2)	
Page 8	Page 1	Page 2	Page 7

Page 5 (front of sheet 3)		Page 6 (back of sheet 3)	
Page 4	Page 5	Page 6	Page 3

Making new pages in Word

If you type past the end of a page in your document, Word will automatically add a new page. However, you can also add new pages by pressing the *Control* key and the *Return* key at the same time. This is useful for keeping bits of text separate from each other as you work.

Gutter

Toes

My toes are like a family,
Five little piggies snuggling up.
A bunch of potatoes in a furrow,
Or maybe like a flower's petals.

A row of walkers on a hill,
One leader and four more behind.
Or else like broad beans in their pod,
Or someone's very short, fat hand.

And yet the lines above are wrong.
My toes are not like anything.
In fact they're just a row of toes,
And all they look like is my toes.

8

Contents

Polar Bear	2
Snoring Patrick	3
The Hurricane	4
Noah's Ark	5
Robin Hood	6
In Winter	7
Toes	8

1

It's easiest to add page numbers by putting each one in its own text box (see page 29).

Remember you can use tabs, alignment and different styles when designing your text.

Book binding

When you've printed the book on both sides of each sheet of paper, fold and arrange them in order with the cover on the outside. Then bind the book by stapling or glueing it together at the fold, or spine. If your stapler doesn't reach, another good way is to use a needle and thread to sew the pages together along the spine.

Sew about three large stitches down the spine.

Book ideas

Here are some ideas for books to make:

Recipe book Put a contents list on page 1 and a different recipe on each of the other pages.

Travel guide Prepare a book about your area for someone who's coming to stay.

Book of poems Collect and type out poems you like, to make an anthology, or make a book of your own poetry.

Picture story book Write a story for a brother or sister, or a child you know. You could even it write about them.

For a smart look, use thick paper or card for the cover.

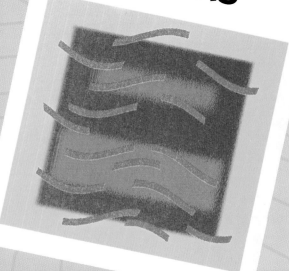

MY BOOK OF POEMS

Design a logo

A logo is a simple picture or symbol that stands for something. Clubs, societies and businesses often have logos, and you can have one too.

This panda logo stands for the WWF, the global environment network.

USBORNE

Usborne Publishing's logo is a colourful hot-air balloon.

Your own logo

You could design a logo for yourself and put it on your letterheads, envelopes, stickers or anything else you want to personalize. Or you could design one for a club, a school or college magazine, or a business.

Ideally, a logo should relate to the thing it stands for. For example, it could contain a set of initials, or it could be a simple picture that symbolizes a person, club or store.

A picture logo for a flower shop

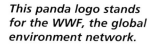

A logo made up of initials

A music group logo

This logo for a drama club is made up of words inside a speech bubble.

Logos in Word

You could just draw your logo using Paint (see page 14) or design it on paper and scan it into your computer (see page 45). But there are lots of ways Word can help you produce a stylish logo.

AutoShapes

The *AutoShapes* menu (see page 17) has lots of shapes which make great logos. When you've drawn your shape, right-click on it and select *Format AutoShape*. Use the AutoShape tools to change the colour, outline colour and thickness.

WordArt

A word or a set of initials can make a great logo if you make them into a WordArt picture (see page 28).

Dingbat fonts

Dingbats fonts like *Dingbats 1*, *Wingdings* and *Astro* are a good source of logos. Just find a picture you like and choose a font size and text colour.

Text logos

Try making a logo using a word or a set of initials in a wacky font. Remember you can also change the style (see page 28). Put your letters in a text box (see page 29) so that you can move them around on the page.

Mix and match

You can use any combination of design techniques in your logos. Word will let you put text inside an AutoShape, or put one AutoShape on top of another. This means you can put any logo inside an outline, or build up your own image out of several different words and shapes.

Logo tips and tricks

• The most important rule of logo design is: keep it simple! Most famous logos are based around a basic shape such as a circle, triangle, square or ellipse.
• Your logo will be most effective if you use just one or two colours.
• For a complete look, use the colours from your logo in other parts of your publication ~ for example, put a rule under your letterhead in the same colour.
• There are so many logos around, it can be hard to make sure yours doesn't look like someone else's. So try to make it unique ~ most famous logos are protected by copyright, which means it's illegal to copy them.
• Want a tilted logo? Click with the right mouse button on your AutoShape or WordArt box, select *Format*, select the *Size* tab, and enter a value (such as 20) in the "Rotation" box.

A brand image

Companies who have logos make sure that everything they produce has the same logo on it. This gives them a corporate or brand "image", which means that the company logo and colours are always easily recognized.

You can give your school, your club, your band or a small business a brand image by using the same logo and colours on all its publications. Here's an example:

Compliments slip, made from A4 or letter paper cut into 3 strips.

Letterhead

You can buy blank business cards stuck to a sheet of card. You design and print them just like stickers (see page 26).

You could make brand stickers too, or even T-shirts (see page 38).

Fashion design

Want to be a fashion designer? It's easy to do your own T-shirt designs and iron them onto a T-shirt using a transfer sheet. Transfer sheets come in packs of about 10 and are fairly cheap. You can also use them on bags, hats, shoes and other fashion gear.

You will need...

It's a good idea to make sure you've got everything before you start. For most T-shirt transfers, you'll need:

Transfer sheets You can use any brand of T-shirt transfer sheet, as long as it's meant for use with a computer printer. Look for them in your computer store.

Inkjet printer You must use an inkjet printer. A laser printer won't work because it will get hot inside and melt the transfer sheet.

A T-shirt Or whatever else you want to decorate, such as a bag, a hat or a pair of jeans. Whatever it is, it must be made of 100% cotton, so that it will withstand a hot iron. It should also be white, or a pale colour like pink or cream, to make the design show up properly.

An iron If it's a steam iron, make sure it has no water in it, because steam will damage the transfer.

Your design

Set up a new Word document that's the same size as the transfer sheets (usually A4 or letter size). You're now ready to create your own fashion moment! Using any of the design skills described in this book, you can design a logo or a message, or just put a picture on your T-shirt. Here are some ideas:

• Make a T-shirt for your band, club or sports team. Design a logo and then add the band, club or team name.
• Make decorative symbols or patterns using dingbats fonts (see page 18) or Word AutoShapes (see page 17).
• Write a funny or fashionable slogan such as Chill Out, Jet Set, or Hippy Chick. Or use your T-shirt to send out a message, such as Girl Power or Go Veggie! You can add a picture as well, to go with the message.
• You can put a photo of yourself, a pet, your home or anything you like on a T-shirt. You'll have to scan the photo into your computer first (see page 45).

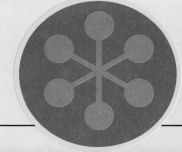

The rocket in this design is made up of Word AutoShapes.

This logo was made using the Dingbats1 font inside an AutoShape.

This Girl Power logo is made up of several Word AutoShapes. The main one has text inside.

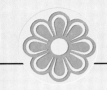

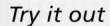

Try it out

When you've finished your design, check it by printing it out on a normal piece of paper and holding it up against your blank T-shirt to see how it will look. To avoid waste, don't print it onto a transfer sheet until you're completely happy with it.

Mirror image T-shirt designs printed onto transfer sheets

Design tips

Remember you'll have quite a lot of space for your design ~ up to the size of the transfer sheet. A small logo or message looks sophisticated, but a big one has lots of impact. Experiment with different effects ~ try putting the design in the middle, at a top corner, or even on the back of the T-shirt.

Printing and ironing

Follow the transfer instructions carefully on how to print out and iron your transfer. In most cases, you'll have to set your printer to "special paper" or "T-shirt transfer", and print a mirror image of your design onto the transfer sheet so that it ends up the right way round. Most printers have an option for doing this. Look in the printer settings for an option called "Flip Horizontal" or "Mirror Image", and select it.

Print your design on a transfer sheet and iron it onto the T-shirt, pressing the iron very hard. Let it cool, then carefully peel it off. If your printer doesn't have this option, print onto good quality paper instead and take it, with a T-shirt, to a printing shop. For a small fee, they'll transfer it for you.

Magazines

If a booklet or newsletter isn't big enough for everything you've got to say, why not design and publish your own full-length magazine?

Plan your magazine

As with a book (see page 34), it's best to make a dummy magazine first, to work out how many pages you need and what will go on each page.

Magazines are usually designed in double-page spreads made up of two facing pages. Usually, one spread will hold one article or story. Or it can be made up of several items in boxes, or lots of small items in columns, such as classified advertisements.

Before using the computer, make a "rough" of each spread by sketching it on paper.

This is a rough for a school magazine spread, containing an interview with a famous writer who came to visit.

Here's a rough for a gossip spread, with photos of people on a day out.

Design decisions

There are several ways of designing and constructing a magazine. Think about the options before you start working in Word.

Small format

You can make a small magazine in just the same way as the book on page 34.

Full-size format

For a bigger magazine you'll need paper twice the normal size, such as A3. If, like many printers, yours won't take paper this big, the easiest thing to do is to design your magazine on smaller paper, as above, making everything smaller than you want it to be. Then enlarge it to twice the size on a photocopier.

Black and white or colour?

If you want to make lots of copies of your magazine, you'll have to photocopy it or send it to a printing shop. Black and white copies are much cheaper than colour, so if you want to save cash, think about making your magazine black and white only. It will still look great if you use interesting fonts and a good layout.

JEDLEY HiGH

The Magazine

Issue No 27

Set up your document

Start a new Word document and set the paper size you're going to print on. Select "Landscape" so that you can put two pages side by side on each sheet. Then hold down the *Control* key and press *Return* to create the number of pages you need.

Remember, you have to put the pages in a particular order in your document, to make them appear in the right order when you print them out and staple or sew the magazine together. (Look at page 34 for a reminder of how to work out the order.) This means you'll be designing half of one spread opposite half of another. For example, in a 16-page magazine, you might be designing pages 7 and 11 opposite each other.

As with a book, print out the finished pages on both sides of the paper, and then assemble them into the right order.

Magazine tips

• **Don't forget the gutter!** Leave a gap in the middle of each page of the Word document, where the stapling will go. Don't put pictures or text in the gutter.
• **Titles and straplines** Use a big, bold font for titles. Then use a smaller font to give a taster of what the article is about. This is called the strapline.
• **Use AutoShapes** Word AutoShapes with text inside are great for funky titles and captions. Ovals and round-cornered boxes look modern. Try a star or thought bubble for a special effect.
• **Columns and breakers** Long pieces of text look best arranged in three columns per page. Jazz them up with breakers ~ mini-headings halfway down the columns.

Gutter

The gang stop for a rest before tackling the tower's 600 steps.

Joe poses for a pic by the railings...

... but Cassie outdoes him in the style stakes!

Debs, Mark and Maria seem to be getting on well!

Check out these pics of the history gang's trip to Tyler Tower!

What they said...

We're having a fantastic time! ~ *Mark and Debs*

Hey! You can see my gran's house from here! ~ *Grant*

I knew I shouldn't have worn these shoes! ~ *Cassie*

I can't look! Hold my hand! ~ *Darren (allegedly)*

Darren keeps smiling, but he's holding on for dear life.

Look out girls! There's a strange man behind you!

We made it to the top! The brave few look down the spiral staircase.

OUR DAY OUT!

What is DTP?

Desktop Publishing software, or DTP, is what most professional graphic designers use to arrange words and pictures together on a computer screen. These two pages explain how it works.

A professional book designer at work using QuarkXPress

DTP programs

The main DTP programs are Quark XPress™, Adobe® Indesign™, Adobe® PageMaker® and Microsoft® Publisher. They are used to design magazines, posters and books (like this one, which was designed using QuarkXPress). DTP software can be expensive. If you want to try it, Microsoft® Publisher is the cheapest and easiest package to begin with.

How DTP works

In DTP, all the text is in boxes (they do not show on the printout). The boxes can be linked together so that text runs from one to another. Pictures and photos are also put in boxes. You can create more complicated shapes and special effects than you can in Word.

A picture in an ellipse

A circle with a colour blend

Curved text...

Stretched text...

This screenshot shows a DTP program being used to design a double-page spread of a book about insects.

Toolbar with edit, rotate, line, box, circle and other tools.

Text and pictures are all in their own boxes.

The designer can control the way the text wraps around the picture.

This red symbol shows there is more text in the box. The box will have to be made bigger to show it all.

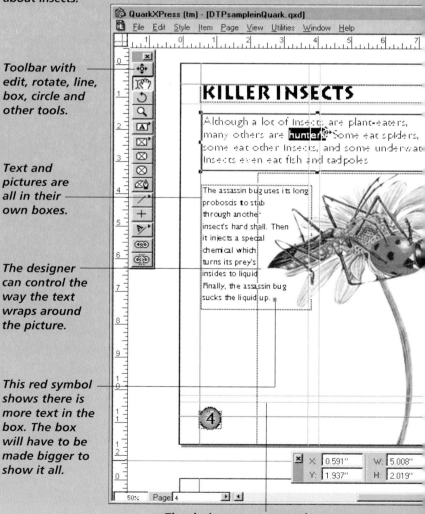

QuarkXPress (tm) - [DTPsampleinQuark.qxd]

File   Edit   Style   Item   Page   View   Utilities   Window   Help

KILLER INSECTS

Although a lot of insects are plant-eaters, many others are **hunters**. Some eat spiders, some eat other insects, and some underwater insects even eat fish and tadpoles.

The assassin bug uses its long proboscis to stab through another insect's hard shell. Then it injects a special chemical which turns its prey's insides to liquid. Finally, the assassin bug sucks the liquid up.

④

X: 0.591"   W: 5.008"
Y: 1.937"   H: 2.019"

50%   Page: 4

The designer can move these green guide rules to any part of the spread.

Image manipulation

As well as DTP software, many graphic designers use programs such as PhotoShop, which allow you to make changes to pictures. For example, using PhotoShop, a designer could make a picture look semi-transparent, create swirls of colour to use as a background, or combine two photos so that one person's head was joined onto another person's body.

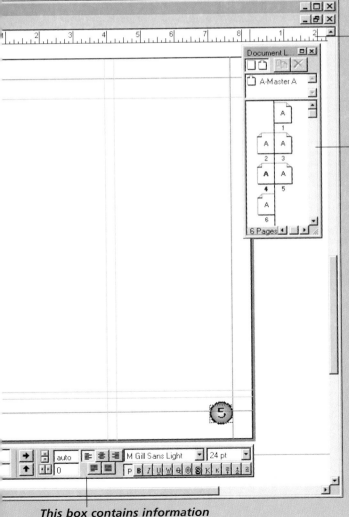

This photo of a girl has been altered in PhotoShop.

The designer has made copies of her arms and attached them to her body, so that she now has four arms.

Rulers along the edges of the screen help with positioning.

This box shows all the pages in the document. The designer clicks here to go to another page.

This box contains information about the highlighted text.

Becoming a designer

Want to be a real graphic designer? You're in luck! Media industries such as magazine publishing, book publishing, advertising and Web site design are expanding at an amazing rate. So, in the 21st century, good designers are more in demand than ever.

If you want to become a graphic designer, it helps to pick art, design and computer-related subjects to study at school. Most designers then study art and design at college or university.

New design programs are always being invented, so working designers sometimes go on courses to help them keep up with the latest technology.

Saving, printing and scanning

These two pages contain some more useful information about saving files in Word, printing your designs, and using scanners.

Saving and naming your file

Each Word document you work on has to be saved, so that you can store it, find it and open it again whenever you want. The first time you save a file, click on *Save* in the *File* menu. A dialog box will appear.

Type the name of your document in this box.

Word will give your document a name such as Doc1.doc, but you can change this to something else, such as Letter.doc or Xmasparty.doc, to make it easier to find again later. Make sure the file name includes the ending .doc, so that your computer will identify it and open it again as a Word document.

Word will also ask you where you want to put your file. You can select a folder on your computer to store it in, or create a new folder for your designs. Finally, click on *Save* to save the file.

When you save the same file again, use the *Save As* command instead, and click on *Yes* to save the new version.

Closing Word

To close Word down, click on *Exit* in the *File* menu, or click on the X symbol in the top right-hand corner of the screen. Make sure you save your file before closing Word.

Printers

There are several types of printers. The cheapest and most common are inkjet printers, which are easy to find in computer stores and often come free with computers. This is the best type of printer for the projects in this book. Laser printers are not recommended, because they get very hot inside, which can damage some types of special paper.

This picture shows a typical inkjet printer and its main parts.

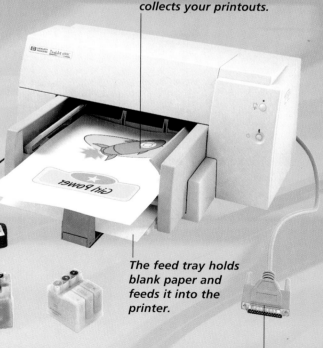

The output tray collects your printouts.

The power cable plugs into a wall socket.

The feed tray holds blank paper and feeds it into the printer.

Most printers take refill cartridges that look like this.

This cable plugs into the back of your computer.

Printer settings

When you buy a new printer, follow the instructions on how to set it up and install the printer software that comes with it.

To print something, click on *File* in the menu bar, and select *Print...* A dialog box for your printer will appear. This lets you set the printer to the right paper size, paper type, number of copies, colour settings and print quality (known as the "resolution"). A high resolution printout will take longer to print. You may need to click on *Properties* to see some of these options.

When you've selected the settings, click on *OK* or *Print* to start printing. With most printers, another dialog box appears during printing. It will have a *Stop* or *Cancel* option so that you can stop printing if you change your mind.

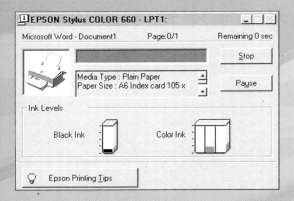

Printer paper

Computer stores sell all kinds of paper and special media for inkjet printers, including letter paper, coloured paper, thin card, photo quality paper, blank business cards, postcards, T-shirt transfers and stickers. Remember that when you print on these, you have to set the printer settings to the right size and paper type, and make sure the feed guides on your printer are set to the right width.

Scanners

A scanner is useful if you want to copy photographs, or your own artwork, into the computer to use in your designs.

This section explains briefly how it works, but remember that all scanners are different. Like printers, they come with their own software and instructions, which you should read carefully.

Scanning an image

The most common type of scanner is a flatbed scanner. This is how it works.

First, you open the lid and place the thing you want to scan face down on the scanner window.

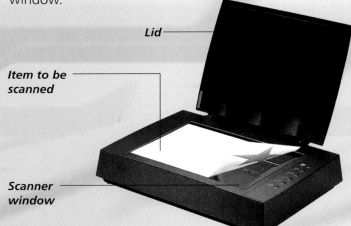

Lid

Item to be scanned

Scanner window

As with a printer, you use the on-screen settings to select the quality, or resolution, of your scan, and to choose colour or black and white. Most scanners do a rough scan first, and show you a preview so that you can move your picture if necessary, or select just one part of it to scan. Once you're sure, you click on *Scan* or *OK* to do the final scan.

You then name and save the image as a picture file. Almost all scanners will let you save it as a .bmp (bitmap) file, which is what you need if you want to import the picture into Word.

Glossary

This page explains some of the unusual design words and computer jargon used in this book.

Alignment The way rows of text line up with each other.

Bitmap (.bmp) A type of computerized picture file which can be used with Word.

Breaker A small heading used to break up a column of text.

CD-ROM A CD containing software or information for use on a computer.

Clicking and dragging Holding down your mouse button while you move the mouse. This method is often used to "drag" objects around on your computer screen.

Clip Art Computerized pictures which can be used in Word documents.

Crash When a computer crashes, it stops working and the screen freezes up or goes blank. To fix it, you need to switch off your computer and restart it.

Desktop PC A large computer that sits on top of a desk.

Dialog box A box which appears on your computer screen to allow you to choose various options or settings.

Digital To do with the way a computer stores information. A digital picture is a picture stored on a computer.

Dingbats Fonts that are made up of little pictures instead of letters and numbers.

Dummy A pretend version of a book, made to help with the design process.

Font A style of lettering. Also known as a **typeface** or **type**.

Graphic design Designing pictures and text for paper or computer publications, such as books, magazines or Web sites.

Icon A small picture used on a computer screen to stand for something.

Internet Service Provider (ISP) A company that handles e-mail and access to the Web. You need an account with an ISP if you want to use the Internet.

Landscape Used to describe any picture which is wider than it is tall.

Laptop A small, portable computer.

Masthead The area of a newsletter or newspaper that contains the title.

Menu A list of options on your computer screen. Sometimes, when you click on one option, a new menu appears.

Modem A device which converts computer information into signals which can be sent down a telephone line.

Notebook Another name for a laptop.

Point size A way of measuring type. One point is 0.35 mm or 1/72 of an inch. This sentence is in 11-point type.

Portrait Used to describe any picture which is taller than it is wide.

Resolution The sharpness of a computer picture, scan or printout.

Rough A rough design sketch.

Sanserif A font without serifs (see below).

Score To cut or press a line into a piece of paper or card to make it fold easily, without cutting all the way through it.

Serif A small, sticking-out tab on a letter of the alphabet. A serif font is a font with letters that have serifs.

Strapline A short sentence which comes after a title to explain briefly what the text is about.

Tab A computer function that inserts a space before the next word you type. Also the name for the parts of a dialog box that you click on.

Thumbnail A small design sketch.

Typeface or **type** Alternative names for a font.

Wrap To make text flow closely around a picture.

Web sites

This page lists Web sites where you can find free fonts and Clip Art pictures. Remember that the Web can change quickly, so don't worry if you can't find all these sites. You can find others by doing a search in any search engine. Use keywords such as "fonts" "Clip Art" and "download" to make sure you find the right kind of site.

Fonts

FreebieSource.com
www.freebiesource.com/fonts.html
Fonts for Kids
home.att.net/~mickeymousemania/fonts.htm
Free Windows Fonts for Kids
www.billybear4kids.com/fonts/fonts.htm

Downloading fonts

Most font sites will explain how to download, or copy, fonts from the Web onto your computer. You usually have to click on the font you want with your mouse. Select *Save this file to disk* in the dialog box that appears. You can then choose a folder on your computer to put the font file in. It's best to put all your fonts in a folder called *Fonts* which you should find under the *Windows* folder.

When you download your font file, it may be compressed, or "zipped", so that it takes up less space. To use it, you need to "unzip" it using a program called Winzip. You can download this from the Web at **www.winzip.com.** This site also explains how to use Winzip to unzip files.

Once a font is unzipped and in your font folder, you will be able to select it from your font list when you're using Word.

Clip Art

Original Free Clip Art
www.free-clip-art.net/index4.shtml
Barry's Clip Art Server
www.barrysclipart.com/ClipArt
Free Clip Art for Kids
www.thekidzpage.com/freekidsclipart/index.htm
Judy's Free Clip Art
members.nbci.com/galaxy777
Three Birds Studio Clip Art
www.countryfriends.org/KWClipArt.html
Clips Ahoy!
www.clipsahoy.com
Clip Art Connection
www.clipartconnection.com/clipart.html

Clip Art on the Web

The sites listed here are just a few of the hundreds and hundreds of Clip Art sites on the Web. When you get to a Clip Art site, you'll probably see a list of different types of pictures, such as Animals, Cartoons, Flowers, Food, People and so on. Click on the one you want, to view the pictures. If there are too many to fit on one screen, there will be a "Next" button which you can click on to see the next screen. When you find a picture you want, click on it and save it on your computer, as described on page 17.

Most Clip Art sites also have lots of links to similar sites. If you can't find the picture you want, just try a different site.

Remember that Clip Art and fonts on the Web belong to the people who designed them and put them there. They are usually happy for you to use them for your own personal designs. But if a site says you can't copy its pictures, then it is illegal to use them and you should look somewhere else.

Index

Acknowledgements

Microsoft® Word 97and 2000, Microsoft® Paint, Microsoft® WordPad, Microsoft® Office and Microsoft®Windows 95, 98, NT and 2000 are either registered Trade Marks or Trade Marks of Microsoft corporation in the United States and/or other countries. Product images, icon images and screen shots of Microsoft products are reprinted by permission from Microsoft Corporation. Every effort has been made to trace the copyright holders of the material in this book. If any rights have been omitted, the publishers offer their sincere apologies and will rectify this in any future editions following notification.

Usborne Publishing are not responsible and do not accept liability for the availability or content of any Web site other than our own, or for any exposure to harmful, offensive, or inaccurate material which may appear on the Web. Usborne Publishing will have no liability for any damage or loss caused by viruses that may be downloaded as a result of browsing the sites we recommend.

First published in 2001 by Usborne Publishing Ltd., Usborne House, 83-85 Saffron Hill, London EC1N 8RT, England. www.usborne.com. Copyright ©2001 Usborne Publishing Ltd. The name Usborne and the devices 🔱😊 are Trade Marks of Usborne Publishing Ltd. All rights reserved. No part of this publication may be reproduced, stored in a retrieval system, or transmitted in any form or by any means, electronic, mechanical, photocopying, recording or otherwise without the prior permission of the publisher. Printed in Spain.

Computer monitor on front cover reproduced with permission of Hewlett-Packard/Beattie Media. "10,000 Clipart" CD cover on page 17 reproduced by permission of greenstreet ©Copyright 2000. Panda logo on page 36 reproduced by permission of WWF-UK. Photos on page 40-41 ©Digital Vision

This edition produced for:
The Book People Ltd, Hall Wood Avenue, Haydock, St Helens WA11 9UL